The Home Edit Guide Book

Guide on Decluttering and Organizing Your Home

Copyright © 2020

All rights reserved.

DEDICATION

Contents

Where to Begin

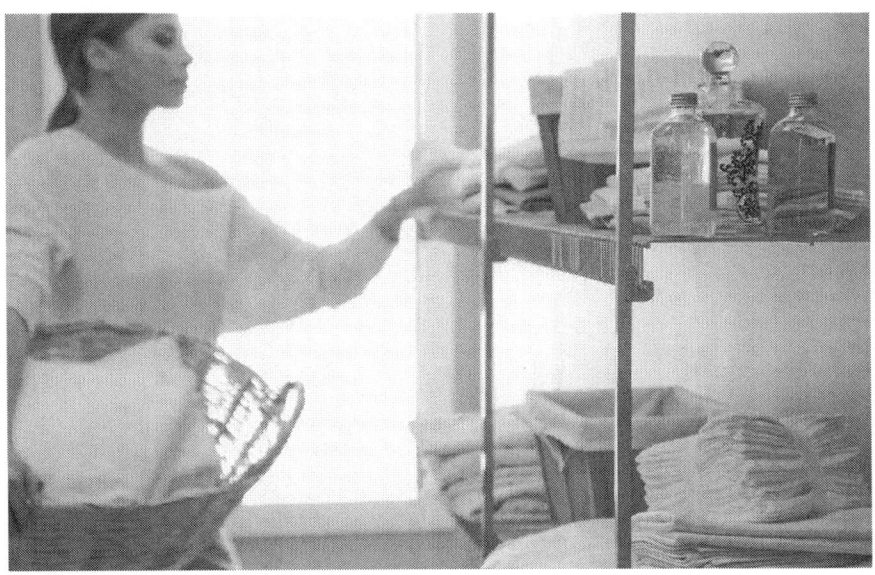

The idea is to create storage space before you tackle the rooms you use most often. This way when you move on to the rooms and spaces you use most, there will be storage space available. This means that when you decide you are not using the Kitchen Aid mixer that's been sitting on your countertop for 5 years, there's a place to store it.

01

of 04

Storage Spaces

Your storage spaces are the place to begin organizing. Once you dive deeper into your house, you're going to be doing a lot of decluttering and rearranging of items. Organize your storage spaces first so that when you find appliances, clothing, shoes, books, and papers that need a place to go, you'll have a place for them. And it will be neat, tidy, and clutter-free.

Think of it like this: Before you unload groceries, you've got to create space for them to go into the fridge. Before you load the dishwasher, you've got to unload the dishwasher.

Start with a project that you can easily complete. Like a junk drawer. Then, move onto a hall closet or a zone in your basement. Break larger spaces up into smaller spaces. For instance, in your basement or attic, tackle one corner, then another. Or one box at a time.

02

of 04

Shared Spaces

Shared spaces should be organized next because they are the most trafficked areas in the home. Start with the kitchen, followed by the foyer, living room and bathrooms.

A big plus to organizing these areas is that if you live with others, they will start to see these spaces organized. Next, they will start to expect these places to be neater which will prompt them to be neater. They may even join in to help you organize. Or they may begin working on their own personal spaces like bedrooms and home offices. Whether they notice or not, organizing is decluttering, sorting, and finding a home for your objects, so before you begin working in shared areas, tell your roommates or family exactly what you're doing, and let them collaborate on the best places to store shared items.

For example, if you have children, let them help you to pick out a storage space for their toys in the living room. As long as you can live with their decision (i.e. it's in a corner, and not in the middle of the room), go with it. They will feel a sense of ownership over the project making them more likely to work with you, not against you.

But, if your fellow house dwellers are resistant, go ahead with your plans. Just make sure they know what goes where when you are done.

Personal Spaces

Personal spaces like bedrooms, closets, and home offices take more concentration to organize. You need to touch and assess most items in these areas to organize the space. That means looking at each paper and examining it, or each grabbing each sock and hunting for its mate.

When organizing the kitchen, you can organize 25 to 40 items at once if you're dealing with utensils. In a closet, you have to make a decision on each button-down shirt, and in an office, you've got to sort each paper and receipt.

These spaces will definitely tax your energy, so it's a good idea to begin these on a weekend morning, with a good cup of coffee or tea.

Don't try to organize a bedroom before tackling the bedroom closet. Closets have a tendency to spill out from behind closed doors very easily. Get them in check before working on your bedroom.

04

of 04

Small Spaces

Now, start on smaller spaces like linen closets, laundry rooms, guest rooms, and mudrooms. These small spaces often get short shrift because they are not very exciting. Yet, having them organized can make your home a more efficient place.

For example, if you have guests coming to visit, having an organized linen closet will make your life a whole lot easier. It will make your guests' visits easier for them as well.

You'll be able to locate extra linens, toiletries, and bathroom supplies, and if you're not around, they can grab these supplies themselves. Likewise, an organized laundry room will make that chore easier by placing the soaps and tools you need front-and-center.

Organize Every Room

Between the kids, adults, and pets in your house, it seems like every room needs a complete makeover. Learn how to organize every room in your family's home, one room at a time, to take charge of the clutter.

Here's a list of rooms with specific tips on how to get started organizing.

01

of 11

Master and Guest Bedrooms

The first room you see in the morning and the last one you see each night doesn't feel like your private oasis anymore. Organize your entire bedroom to make it one of your favorite rooms in the house again. Transform your closet or dresser from looking like a bargain bin into looking like a fancy department store display. Once you've eliminated the mess, rejuvenate the master and guest bedrooms with a deep cleaning top to bottom.

02

of 11

Kids's Bedrooms

We love 'em but the sweet, adorable people who live in these rooms aren't known for being neat freaks. Fortunately, there are some organization tips just for kids' rooms that help you tackle the layer of toys on the floor and messy beds that never get made.

Having some sense of organization helps keep the mess to a minimum even when little hands want to yank today's wardrobe off their hangers. Toys can be neatly organized in your kids' bedrooms so that you're not spending every day re-cleaning the same old mess. You'll actually be able to walk into your child's room and not feel the pain of Legos underneath your feet.

03

of 11

Kitchen

There's a lot of action in the kitchen and it's evident by the crumbs, food stains, and general clutter. If this kitchen was in a restaurant would you want to eat there or would you call the health department to shut it down?

Organize the kitchen in a way that maximizes your counter space and reduces your counter clutter as well as the clutter hidden away in drawers. A clean and organized kitchen makes the entire house feel clean and organized, even when it's not.

04

of 11

Family Room

You're a functional family but you've got a dysfunctional family room. Toys, video games, remote controls, and more end up scattered about—and one of the rooms you spend the most time in becomes one you're constantly cleaning. Do this room in stages to make the room work for you and get rid of the junk pileups.

The task can feel overwhelming, so work with the parts of the room that are bugging you the most first. Set up areas for smaller kids to play in the room to contain their toys. Tidy up the electronics and hold your family to following your system. Thin out the room of anything that doesn't belong there.

05

of 11

Playroom

That mysterious space underneath the toys is called a floor. Haven't seen it in a while, have you? You're not alone. Families everywhere are tired of cleaning up the room that's been designated as the kids' play place, but you can end playroom clutter in an afternoon. Sort toys, organize those that still get used, then donate gently used toys that no one plays with anymore to worthy organizations. Make sure your playroom stays tidy with strategies that include baskets and bins. Try to reassess what your child is playing with regularly so you'll know what to keep the next time you swap out toys or get items ready to donate.

06

of 11

Bathroom

It's easy for the bathroom to get cluttered and dirty because you have tiny people learning how to use the potty, towels hanging everywhere from daily baths, and shampoo, toothpaste, and other personal care items that have to live in this space, too. Grab a box and clean everything out of the bathroom. Everything. Organize your bathroom by starting with a clean slate. Slowly put what you need back in and get rid of everything else.

07

of 11

Garage

The garage is supposed to be a place where we park cars and maybe work on a weekend project using a workbench. It only takes five easy steps to get your garage organized. Take a second look at your garage.

What do you really need in there and what can be thrown out? Hang bikes on the wall so they're not on the floor. Use storage shelves to organize the tools, beach toys, and car supplies vertically. Throw out those empty bottles of brake fluid, the car-washing brushes with worn-out bristles, and broken toys you've been meaning to fix for years.

08

of 11

Mud Room/Laundry Room

Dirty shoes and clothes are left here so, although this room is usually small, it can feel like a gigantic mess. Plus, most mud rooms or laundry rooms have feet constantly walking through them because it's the room where you enter and exit the house. You don't want these areas to look like a drop-off point for everything from the mail to your diaper bag.

09

of 11

Home Office

Whether you use your home office as a homeschool area or to prepare presentations for the board room, this is one of the easiest rooms to load with clutter. Bills end up here, file folders are strewn about, and that big desk makes the perfect tabletop for piling mail, catalogs, and books. Take baby steps to organize this room and begin with a shakedown of the things you don't need anymore.

10

of 11

Hall Closet

Open your hall closet door right now. Happy with what you see? Everyone's hall closet is different but most of us can relate to the hodgepodge of clutter that lurks behind that door. You can maximize the space and minimize the junk factor when you organize closets. Empty the closet, take stock of what you have and make the closet efficient with hooks and organizers to keep your items neatly arranged. Next time you go to grab your coat, you won't have a mini yard sale staring back at you.

11

of 11

Attic/Storage Room

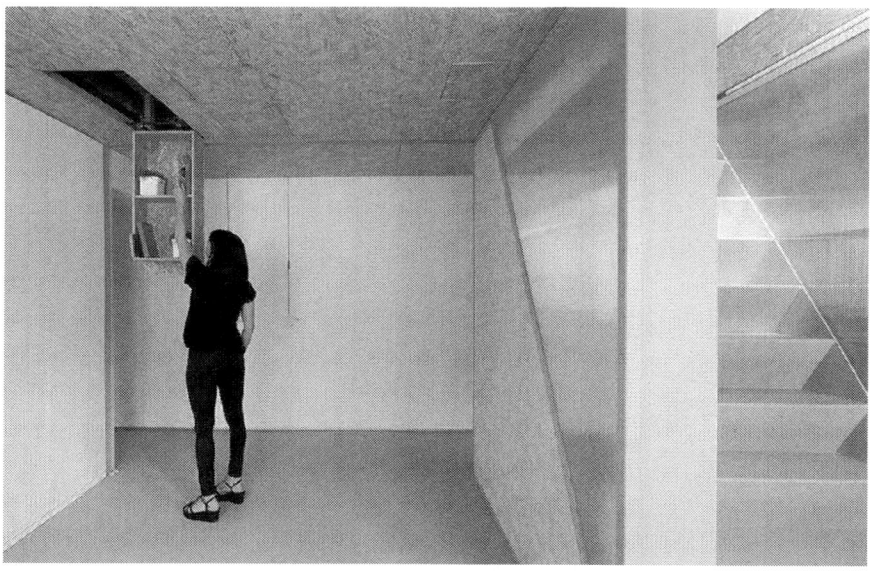

The name of the room says it all. After all, you've probably made your attic or storage room the dumping ground for things you just didn't know what to do with. You know you need to dig in and throw some things out, but the thought of opening the door and having random boxes fall down on you isn't a way you'd like to spend your

Saturday. Assess the space to see how it can be reconfigured for optimal organizational purposes. Don't be afraid to take some items straight to the street. If you haven't needed that box from your bachelorette pad you rented almost 20 years ago, chances are, you won't even miss it.

Room-by-Room Organization Guide

The Organization Equation

Organization is an equation that factors in time, space, money, and effort. When we're organizing with ADHD, we give the greatest value to time and effort. Efficiency is our battle cry. We want the fewest number of steps and the least amount of effort. Otherwise, even if we clear the clutter once, we won't keep it up. Follow this guide on how to organize your home (for good!), room by room.

1. Remember the 3 Rs

To get and keep things in order, use these guiding principals in each room of your home:

Reduce what you have. It's the most direct path to efficient organizing.

Be resourceful. When you have less, you find more creative ways to use your belongings.

Be resilient. If you find you don't have something you need, don't get bent out of shape or rush out to buy more.

2. Inventory Your Kitchen

Eliminate excess Tupperware. It's better to let a drumstick roll around in a too-big container than it is to have 50 plastic boxes with no matching lids clogging your cabinet and refrigerator. Use plastic wrap, zip close bags, or tin foil if you run out. Or eat your leftovers to free up more.

Get rid of different sized plates and bowls, and buy a uniform set. When all of the dishes are the same, it's easy to load and empty the dishwasher or draining rack. You never have to move a dish to get to another dish.

3. You Don't Need So Many Shoes

How do you keep shoes organized without making the system so overwhelming it's ignored? For people without ADHD, stacks of clear shoe boxes might work. For us, we take one at the bottom of the pile, don't put it back and soon the whole room is littered with shoes again. Instead, reduce the shoes you own to a number that will fit in the back of the closet in one row. Then, when you open the door, kick the ones you're wearing inside. Simple and easy to maintain.

4. Expose Your Garbage Cans

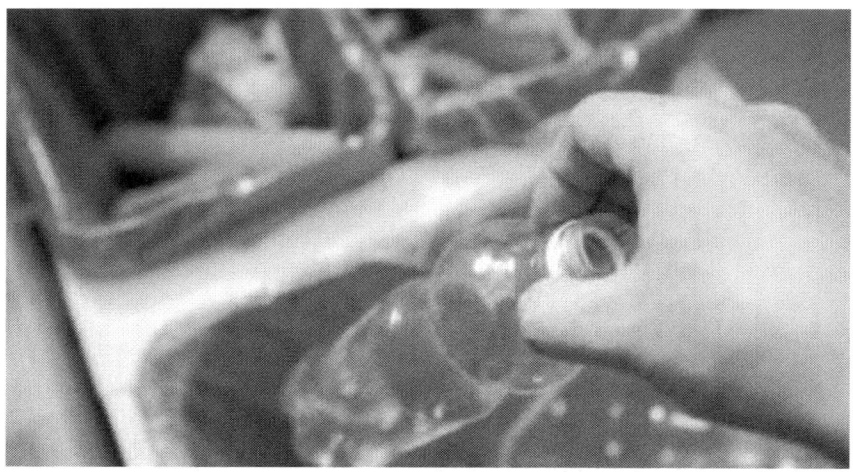

If your family is leaving trash around the kitchen or living room, make it more convenient to throw away. Some families have cans under a cabinet, with a child lock, with a top that only opens halfway. Take the trash can out, put it in a central location and remove the lid. It's not as pretty, but is litter on the counters any better? The goal is to reduce the effort needed for finishing steps — like cleaning up after cooking — so they are a short and workable sprint. It's easy to remember to toss something out when the bin is right in front of you.

5. Streamline Your Socks

Just thinking about laundry is enough to make you groan. First you sort it, then you wash it, then you sort it again only to fold it and put it away. To avoid towering laundry piles, save yourself some steps. Start by getting rid of all of your socks, and buying new ones in only the two colors you wear most often. You'll never have to match and roll socks again.

6. Don't Shred It All

Instead of shredding anything with an account number on it, only eliminate papers with a Social Security number.

Put a bin in your office and your child's homework space that you'll empty just once a year. Unload any paid bills or just-in-case receipts in a stack. Have kids put finished homework there as well. Since the papers lay flat, they won't take up too much space. Then, if you need to go back and look something up, it's there waiting, and filed chronologically.

7. Prioritize the Playroom

Put toys like LEGOs in bins that are shallow and wide, so kids don't have to dump them all out to find the one they want. Get rid of excess toys. When your kid has fewer, he'll play with certain ones more. When they break you can purchase new ones. Cutting back keeps them interested, and your house uncluttered. Then, set a timer for three minutes, and have kids race to see how much they can pick up in that time. You'll be surprised!

8. Heed the Golden Rule

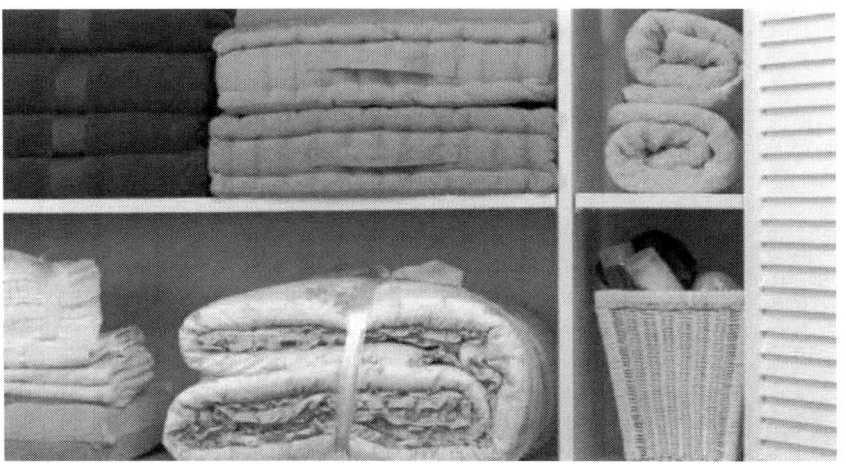

The golden rule of organizing is that inventory must conform to storage. Your goal should be empty shelf and drawer space. Schedule a time on your calendar, go through each room in your home, and reduce. Start with the floors, then move to surfaces, then empty out drawers and interiors. A bedroom will take two days, kitchens take three. If you need help the first time, hire a professional organizer for one project. The skills you learn may be enough to get you through the house.

9. Take 3 Minutes Each Day

There is no organizational system in the world that will work if it's not maintained. Aim for a system, or level of belongings, that will let you pick up any room in three minutes. Then, after dinner, have the family pitch in with clean up. Before sitting down for TV or relaxation time, walk around and put everything away so you're not leaving it until just before bed when you're too tired to move.

10. Less Is More

If you're going to reduce the items in your home so you can clean up in three minutes, don't bring excess into the house. Make it a rule that nothing is purchased that is not on the shopping list. If you're at the store and think you might need milk, don't buy it if it's not on the list. It saves having excess products, and it encourages your family to be resilient by eating toast instead of cereal. If you are at the store and see a buy one, get one half off deal, don't do it unless you have two on your list. Get out of the habit of tying up your money, space, and effort in a bunch of items you don't need or can't use before their expiration date.

11. Set a Routine

It's too much to reinvent the wheel every day. Instead, create systems that support your newly organized life. Make Wednesday bill-paying day. It will avoid paper pile-up on your desk, and make it easier to remember. If you forget one week, when the next Wednesday rolls around, you'll have a sense of urgency to do it. And then, you can relax the rest of the week because you'll know you have a set time to pay bills.

12. Use Supports

Use a timer to help your child clean his room. Hire a neighborhood kid to help you clean the garage. At work, team up with someone who can dot the i's and cross the t's on all of your creative ideas. When you are looking for systems to streamline your home, ask yourself, "Is it efficient? How much work does it take? Can I do it in one step?" Use this guide as a template, and adjust it and customize it to fit your life.

Monthly Home Organization Calendar and Checklist

This monthly home organization checklist will take you from January to December and provide a home organization project and resources and ideas of how you can get your home organized each month. By following this calendar, you can get your home organized the old fashioned way: working a little bit at a time, tackling big projects each month. If you need extra motivation to keep your house clutter free all year, you can combine this with the weekly organizing routine to keep your home neat, tidy and clutter free.

Below you'll find some of the best ways to stay organized month to month.

01

of 12

January: the Closet

January means a fresh start, and we like to start with the biggest challenge in most homes: the closet. Whether you spend a few evenings a week or one entire Saturday on this task, you're going to feel like a new person when you're done.

02

of 12

February: Kitchen

The closet, which we tackled in January, may present the biggest challenge, but the kitchen tends to have the most clutter. Think about all of those appliances, pots, pans, cooking utensils and piles of paper clutter! Take a deep breath, and we'll work through the process again in your kitchen: clean, declutter, store and maintain your new organization.

03

of 12

March: Paper, Mail, and Finances

Organizing paper, mail, and finances in March will mean fewer headaches in April. Now that we had the right mail management system set up that we follow each week, we find paper management to be a very grounding process.

04

of 12

April: Bathroom

Nothing will get your day off to a better start than a clean, well-organized bathroom, and nothing will make hosting guests easier than a well-organized linen closet. Start by decluttering these spaces by tossing old toiletries and medications, and then donating old linens to an animal shelter. If that old sheet set is too ratty for a guest to use, it's not good enough for you, either.

05

of 12

May: Shoes + Boots

It's time to get back into the closet to store winter clothes, donate what you didn't wear this season, and re-arrange for spring and summer. It's also time to delve into organizing shoes and boots. Since you already organized your closet in January, you'll have a little extra time to work on your shoe collection

06

of 12

June: Garages

Garages, with their combination of tools, sporting equipment, appliances, beach gear, bikes and even sometimes, cars, are an easier job than you think. The trick is to think like a department store manager and organize your garage into zones, much like a department store is organized. This makes so much sense, we almost look forward to this yearly task.

07

of 12

July: Clothes

We hit the clothes in January, now is a good time to go back in and organize your clothes. This means a lot of decluttering. Think about donating or consigning clothing, shoes, and accessories that you no longer wear. it's also a good time to repair winter or fall clothing.

08

of 12

August: Daily Routines

We've gone over paper clutter, mail management and personal finances earlier in the year. This month, let's go back through each of those systems. How are they working for you? Do you need to re-adjust?

This month we'll add in daily routines. Do you follow the same routine each day? A routine can be a very powerful weapon in the fight for productivity, and they can be customized to your life.

09

of 12

September: Linen Closets

September is the month of prep work. You should begin organizing linens, linen closets, bathrooms, and guest bedrooms without the threat of guests arriving at your door any minute. Take the time now to carefully declutter and clean these areas so they are working for you when holiday guests arrive. Think about donating old linens to a shelter, purging your guest bedroom of old clothing and donate it, and go through and toss old medications, toiletries and makeup.

10

of 12

October: Pantries, Cabinets, and Drawers

This month's big project is going to take some decluttering but you'll be glad when it's done. it's time to get your pantry, cabinets, and drawers organized and clutter-free.

11

of 12

November: Holidays + Kitchen Prep

Wondering how to deal with the calm before the storm with the holidays and kitchen prep? We're heading back into the kitchen, and this time we'll work on pulling serving dishes, utensils, and China out of the cabinet for inspection. This is also the time to organize your food storage containers since you'll be handing out or receiving holiday leftovers and baked goods in the coming months.

12

December: Clutter

No heavy lifting in December, it's all about purging your home of clutter and then donating the useful, clean and well-made items to a worthy cause. We like the juxtaposition of clearing your home before you receive new items this time of year, and before you welcome in the new year. You need to clear out the old before you can receive the new. If you're one of those people who has a hard time letting go, fear not: we've got a ton of resources to help you with this process.

Tips

Set up a no-fail garage system

Here's an approach that's simple, inexpensive, and quick to accomplish.I suggest starting out in the garage, because it can be one of the most overcrowded places in the house. Picture yourself driving into your garage and seeing at least one new system set up for easy use in the coming year.

Hang some peg board

Put some tool hooks in the holes on the board

Using a thick marker, draw an outline around each tool to reserve its location.

Your new tool organizing system will keep you organized, and alert you when tools are missing. This garage system also helps other family members put things away because it's easy to see where to place each item.

Cut laundry time in half

How can one of the smallest rooms in the house seem so chaotic? And why does doing laundry seem to take up so much time?

Here's a laundry system that will save you time and restore your sanity. First, provide everyone with their own laundry basket. Put family members' names on the sides of the baskets so there are no lost items or mix-ups.

Now here's the sweet secret. When the wash is done, rather than placing the clean laundry on the dining room table or the stairs (and watching everyone walk by without picking up their clothes), have everyone come to the laundry room to pick up their personalized basket of clean clothing.

Work some kitchen magic

The kitchen is the activity hub of most homes. It's a busy area because family members or roommates use the kitchen at least three to five times a day. We open our mail here, study, read, use our laptops and tablets here — not to mention, it's where the food is.

Because we have so many varied activities happening in the kitchen, it's wise to create separate stations for those activities. One way to accomplish this is to invest in a rolling cart — whatever style and size works best in your kitchen.

Use this cart to establish a dedicated space for one of your most common activities. For example, create a lunch-making station stocked with a cutting board and knife, salt and pepper, paper towels, and non-perishable food items (bread, oranges and apples) and snacks. Create the space for your family to assist in making your life easier while also keeping one station of like-items together.

Put it in writing

Whether you're a one-person household or a family of five, one tool can save your life or home: a household manual. The beauty of this handy tool is it doesn't have to be compiled all at one time, and it costs you nothing to create.

Grab a three-ring binder and a three-hole punch, and keep your essential information in the binder. To get started, collect your emergency contact info and other vital information such as the name of your vet, school rosters, alarm codes, medication doses for your kids, the name of your father's caregiver, and where your home's gas shut-off valve is located.

As you continue to organize your home and find more essential documents, you can add to the binder. For those who prefer a digital approach, store your manual on a highly secure cloud service.

Get a charge

Many people are frustrated by cell phones, iPad chargers, memory sticks and tangled cords sprinkled throughout the house. Relaxation and recreation activities often seem to need the power of a charging station that's easily accessible — and it doesn't hurt if it's attractive too.

One simple solution is to consider a charging station that conceals the cords, keeps all the electronic items together, and looks good while doing it.

Tell a tidier toy story

Whether it's grandparents or new moms and dads, one of the biggest complaints of people who share their home with children is about picking up toys.

The "putting away" task is a skill that can and should be taught to children, as it's important for establishing personal responsibility in kids as they grow into teens and then adulthood. Besides, putting away toys can be fun.

Here's one idea that will shift your play storage situation from frustration to elation. Use colorful bins to hold toys, designating each bin to hold one type of toy, such as musical instruments, cars, dolls, games or Legos.

To make it even easier, find pictures of the toys in magazines or online, and use them to label the bins.

If you have dolls or stuffed animals in one bin, attach the matching picture to the front of the bin. Keep the number of bins small, but make sure the bins are large and easy to access.

Declutter the grownups' bedroom closet

Bulging closets and growing piles of clean and dirty laundry may nix the possibility of either rest or romance. Decluttering in the bedroom creates a sanctuary for both.

Starting with the closet is good move. Once the space is clear, it all boils down to finding what you need when you need it.

Here's a quick process for getting your closet in order:

Clear the floor so you can move around easily.

Make sure you have proper lighting.

Pull everything out.

Only put back in what fits you right now, is stain-free, and requires no repairs.

Set kids' closets straight

For organizing kids' clothes, there's no better tool than a hanging shelving unit. Designate one pocket for each day of the week, and label it. Each weekend, pick out clothes for the following week, and put them in the pockets for the day your child will wear them. Imagine a calm morning without clothing conflict.

Bundle toiletries and grooming tools

Some bathrooms are small, and everyone seems to have their own favorite shampoo, hairbrush and brand of toothpaste. Drawer, cabinet and counter space tends to run out quickly.

If this is your situation, try assigning everyone in the house a bathroom caddy, loaded up with all their cosmetics, toiletries and grooming tools, and labeled with their name.

Store the caddies on a shelf in the bathroom or carry them to and from the bedroom. The bathroom stays organized, and there's an automatic clean-up built in after every visit.

Simplify — and go easy on yourself

Eliminating clutter is the best thing you can do to make your home feel more manageable. Less clutter means less stuff to clean and organize in the first place; take just 10 minutes today, and eliminate 10 items you no longer need.

Most importantly, don't get too hung up on the details. Your home doesn't have to be perfectly organized every day. Sometimes "good enough" is just fine.

Made in the USA
Coppell, TX
30 November 2020

The 21 day Self-Love Challenge

learn how to love yourself unconditionally, cultivate self-worth, self-compassion and confidence

21 Day Challenges

ISBN-13: 978- 1514315194
ISBN-10: 151431519X

The 21-Day Challenges

Happiness

Self-love

Self-Confidence

Mindfulness

Stress Management

Minimalism

Productivity

Budgeting

Exercise

Weight Loss

Clean Eating

Introduction

I would have started this book with an earnest question - do you suffer from low self-esteem? - but I already know the answer. Why? Because *most people* have a low self-esteem. And of course they do. We live in a world where we call people who love themselves arrogant, where we encourage children to compete with one another in school and where we immerse ourselves daily in media of all the millions of things we have to do before we are considered adequately lovable.

Low self-esteem, low confidence, self doubt, self hatred, shyness, guilt, shame, soul-crushing depression - call it whatever you want, the idea is the same: you, the person whose opinion should matter to you the most, *don't accept yourself.*

Low self-esteem isn't just High School girls arguing over who is fatter. It's much more serious than this, and can have pretty devastating consequences. See if you can find yourself in any of the following statements. If you can, then read right on - this book was written for you.

- You often worry about what other people think of you (and surprise! You usually assume that their thoughts are bad...)

- You feel that when compared to your peer group, you're "falling behind".

- You frequently embark on "fix up" projects for your life. This could be a promise that no, seriously, you're really going to go to the gym already, or a makeover, or splashing out on fancy supplements or $400 worth of self help audio books from this Indian swami you found on the internet.

- You feel crushed by negative criticism. Completely crushed. Your whole day can be ruined if the cashier doesn't laugh at your joke.

- In the same way, the minute someone praises you, you're on top of the world again.

- You can think of a few things in your life that you're too old / fat / shy / lazy / uneducated / whatever to try. So you just dream about it instead.

- You binge on bad food, smoke, take substances or drink more than you know you should, thinking in the back of your mind, "so what if I get liver damage? It's just me, who even cares."

- You often find yourself bullied, manipulated, coerced or going along with stuff you don't really want to do.

- Deep down, you feel like everyone else is a little better than you.

- You dream of a point far in the future where finally, *finally* everything will be better and you won't suck as much as you do now.

Wow! That was depressing. But, did any of those seem all too familiar? If so, read on. We're about to embark on a journey through - and out of - this kind of senseless self hate, one day at a time. Are you ready?

Day One : Where you are now

Yes yes yes, you've heard it all before. The relentless, never-ending chore: be happy with yourself! Love yourself! Be true to who you are! It used to be that fashion magazines only ever pressured you to change up your hair or buy new shoes, but they're worse these days. Not only do you need to look gorgeous, be perfect in bed and cook your beautiful children 5 star healthy meals worthy of a Pinterest board, you have to be a strong, independent woman who loves her stretch marks, celebrates her curves and is besties with her "true self."

Sigh. The list is never-ending. So we buy self help books, try to squeeze in a meditation class after work and before dinner, and get into the worthless habit of telling our friends, "you're beautiful!" even though we don't mean it in the slightest.

Somewhere along the line some ladies at Dove decided to strip down to their padded bras and undies and proclaim flawless self-love. The word "curvy" became a staple and it became the fashion to tell heart-warming tales of self-acceptance, a-ha moments and you-go-girl positive energy.

So... is it working? Do you love yourself already, dammit?!

I'm going to start this book off on a cynical note and guess that you don't.

What is self-love?

Good question. Perhaps a good place to start would be to say that in this book, we'll abandon the fashion magazine concept of self-love. For many people who've been raised to quietly hate themselves like it's the most natural thing in the world, "self-love" seems kind of ...arrogant. *Love* yourself? How indulgent!

Here, self-love doesn't mean you don't love anyone else, it doesn't mean you're selfish, it doesn't mean you eat all the birthday cake and it doesn't mean you get to flounce off when someone rightly criticizes you. Self-love doesn't mean you're perfect, or that you've solved all your problems. It's not a reward you get after you've unlocked a special awesomeness level in the game of life. And it isn't something you just tick off the list once and for all.

Do you love yourself?

It's a simple question. Try this experiment: ask someone you know, "hey, do you love yourself?" and see what they say. Really, go and do it. I'll wait.

You didn't do it did you? That's fine, I think I can guess the answers you got anyway:

"Love myself? Yeah, I guess I do. I mean, I wouldn't say 'love' or anything, but..."
"Nah"
"Love myself? You mean, like, am I confident?"
"What are you talking about?"
"What's your definition of self-love, though?"
"Maybe sometimes"
"Not really"

Ask ten people and I can guarantee that none of them will give you a straightforward "yes". They'll look at you as though you just asked them what the sound of one hand clapping is, or say yes but follow it with a bunch of disclaimers. I'm betting your answer is similar. You love yourself when you're particularly lovable. You'll get around to self-love once you stop being such a loser. Self-love? Yeah yeah, you'll put it on the list.

Today, I want you to try and remember your answer to this question. By the end of the book, I'm hoping it will be ...a little different. Make a note somewhere of your self-love score from 1 to 10.

(Before we continue - what do you think would have happened if you asked those same people, "do you love your children?" or "do you love your wife?")

Day Two: Why is it so difficult to say " I love you" to yourself?

People love a lot of things. They love their grannies and they love spring and they love peanut butter cups and they love cats on the internet. They Love New York and they love you, boop boop bedoop! For most people, it's easy to throw around this word "love".

But picture yourself for a moment at the gym with a friend after an intense racquetball game. Picture your friend in the changing rooms, smiling at his reflection in the mirror and saying, "I just love my butt!"

Assuming you don't think he's joking, what do you think?

Presumably, this man's butt is just one of the many lovable things in the world, and certainly more lovable than some of the other things people confess their love for (why do people like pugs? I've never understood it). Presumably there's also someone out there who thinks this man's butt is just fabulous, and we can be sure his mom would never say an unkind word about it. Is his butt really all that loveable? Who knows.

The point is, you might think, "oh my god what a narcissist" or, if you're feeling particularly nasty, "his butt isn't even that nice."

Why?

Why is our immediate response to self-love so negative? Chances are, you'd never say something like that about yourself either. The cultural assumption seems to be that it's fine to hate yourself loudly in public, but you'll get stares if you do something as outrageous as give yourself a compliment.

Today, make a note somewhere or simply meditate on the reasons why you feel uncomfortable being kind and loving to yourself. Here are some common reasons, but you can add your own:

I can't love myself because:

- I'm so imperfect and have so much improvement to do.

- I don't deserve it, period.

- It's not ladylike to be so boastful.

- That's just lame hippie nonsense.

- I don't want to make other people feel bad.

- I'm a realist; I don't live in la-la land.

- Other people don't love me, why should I love myself?

Ouch. That last one hurt. But be honest. If you said to yourself, "hey, you're alright" in the gym changing rooms, what would that feel like?

Day Three: Unraveling misconceptions about self-love

What if I told you all of those reasons mention yesterday are based on misunderstandings of what self-love actually is?

It might seem funny coming from a self help book, but I sincerely believe that a lot self-improvement literature out there is, well, it's *crap*. The constant message of "be better be better be better" has a darker, hidden message: you only get to be happy once you're better. You only get to love yourself once you've lost weight or once you've gotten rid of your negative thinking. Perversely, you only get to love yourself after you've read a book about it and "earned" it.

Look, I love a good excuse as much as the next person, but I'm going to go and kill each one of them right here. Ready?

I'm not perfect / good enough yet

So what? Are the people you love in your life perfect? Self-love isn't a reward.

I don't deserve it

When it comes to kind, loving acceptance, there is no "deserve". We're all human, we all suck a little bit, but we're also all trying. In fact, it's those that don't "deserve" love who deserve it the most.

I don't want to be boastful

Cool, I don't want you to be boastful either. Luckily, self-love has nothing to do with being arrogant. Saying "I love you" isn't the same thing as saying "You're perfect and better than everyone else".

I'm not a hippy

Confession: I sort of am. I hope you can still love me! Anyway. I also hope that the rest of this book convinces you that self-love is just a normal thing that has real, tangible effects in the world.

I don't want to make other people feel bad

This one makes me sad. Love isn't a zero sum game and loving yourself doesn't mean there's less for everyone else. In fact, sometimes the one thing you need to convince you to love yourself is to see someone else brave enough to do it.

Self-love isn't realistic

This is just a big old serious grown up way of saying, "I'm not lovable!" The prospect of you being kind and accepting of who you are is realistic, I assure you.

Other people don't love me, so how can I love myself?

Ah, the painful one. If this is you, I want you to hold onto those feelings of being unlovable and unworthy - eventually, my hope is that you realize they don't belong to you and can be released. For now, I want you to try and believe that even if it's true that you are fundamentally unlovable (hint: it's not), you can *still* love and respect yourself.

Day Four: Visualize

To be honest, I think that simply visualizing something is not enough (alright, maybe I'm not such a hippy after all!). My unpopular opinion: just sitting on your ass imagining that things are better can actually be more harmful to you actually reaching your goals. Your brain is fooled into thinking that something has actually changed, and you make no real movements towards improvements.

But, one exception to this is with emotions. This is because when you "visualize" emotions, you are not just imagining them. You're *doing* them. You cannot imagine an emotion without feeling it, at least a little. Poor self-esteem and lack of belief in your worth as a person are not rooted in facts and logic. They're rooted in emotions. And visualization exercises are ways to "practice" having *different* emotions.

So here, visualization is not just conjuring up a pretty picture in your mind and hoping that through some mysterious universe juju it will land in your lap. If that were true I wouldn't be writing this book and would instead be off on my yacht right now, entertaining my billionaire fiancé over a glass of champagne. But I digress.

Today's exercise: visualizing, aka "practice".

Because most of us have had so much practice thinking the worst possible things of ourselves, our neurons have literally wired themselves up for it. The only way to break away is to *be willing to think something else*. When you visualize, you don't have to believe it 100% at first. You're just giving your mind a chance to try out something ...different. You're just opening up a little window.

Whether it's in a journal, through a chat with someone you trust or just something you meditate on, imagine how your life would be if you loved yourself. Have fun with this. I find that the people who are most trapped in their conceptions about themselves have the most fabulous imaginations of us all.

Imagine yourself without self-doubt, self-hate and poor self-esteem. Imagine yourself braver, more trusting, freer, more spontaneous, more relaxed. Imagine yourself out there in the world, sharing who you are with others. Picture yourself with an unshakable confidence, a rock solid self-esteem and the ability to bounce back from failure and criticism, not crumpled but better for it.

If you loved yourself, what would you do differently?
Who would you be with if you had this 24 karat self-esteem?
What habits would you have that you don't have now?
Which habits do you have now that wouldn't fit your calm, self-loving self?

I'm not going to tell you, "ok now go and do all that!"

No, for now, just practice how it feels to think of yourself differently. Just try on the mind of someone who loves themselves.

Day Five: Commit to self-love

Ok, *now* I'm going to tell you to just go and do it.

Note down somewhere three key areas that have emerged for you as places you need to work on. Perhaps, as you did your visualizing yesterday, you uncovered that feeling bad about yourself means you allow other people to treat you badly, too. In this case, "relationships" will be one of your three areas.

Maybe you discover that your focus is on harmful eating habits ("If I loved myself, I wouldn't pack away a bacon-wrapped deep fried whole cheesecake with sprinkles every evening"). Maybe you would have the guts to go out and buy that fancy pair of salsa shoes you've been eyeing. Oh, and sign up for salsa classes.

Whether you're a fan of traditional marriage or not, there's a lot to be said about that moment when you decide, "yes, I'm committed to this."

Commitment doesn't mean a promise to be perfect, it just means that you're willing to put in the work. Whenever you want things to be different from the way they are now, expect resistance. Expect your unconscious mind to come up with a million colorful ~~reasons~~ excuses for why you can't.

If it hasn't already, that little voice has probably poked its stupid head up: "Are you *sure*? Better self-esteem? Whatever. I mean, it's *you* we're talking about. I can see how that might work for someone who's not so terrible but let's be honest, you suck for a reason, am I right?"

Your job in committing is not to stop having this resistance, only to dedicate yourself to seeing it and carrying on anyway. All change requires a little discomfort. Today, make some special vows to yourself. This is not some silly schoolgirl crush we're talking about - you're committing to loving yourself through thick and thin. Some days, that'll be hard. Other days, it'll be the most natural thing in the world. But, there's no relationship as important as the one you have with yourself, so make the commitment. Stick to it.

Today's goal: write your marriage vows - to yourself.

Day Six: Self-care

Let's stick with the marriage metaphor for a little bit. On day one, I suggested to ask people if they loved themselves, and then compare their answers with whether they love their mom, their husband or their pet salamander.

Even people with really tattered self-esteem can still find love for those around them. Have you noticed, in fact, that the same new mom who would kill someone with her bare hands if they threatened her child would have no problem berating herself for having cottage cheese thighs and bags under her eyes.

This is day one of your new marriage to yourself, and remember, *you committed*. So, be nice.

Think about it: would you ever tell your spouse that you hated their guts and that they weren't worthy of your affection (if yes ... uh, this is perhaps not the most urgent book you should be reading)? Would you ignore them most of the time and tell them to suck it up when they got sick? Would you expect them to work hard, never rest and never do the things they enjoyed and grew them as a person?

The reason I'm framing things this way is because it's so easy to see the importance of self-care ...when it's for someone else.

Even better, think of *baby* you. If a baby is crying do you tell it to get a grip and that you'll only love it as soon as it gets its life together? When you tell yourself, "I'll have self-love just as soon as I get my degree" or "I'll have better self-esteem once I lose weight", picture saying the same thing to a person you love, to your husband or wife, to a young you. Does it still seem right?

If you've ever crowed about "unconditional love", well, try give yourself some. Self-love is active and luckily, it's actually pretty fun to do. Actions speak louder than words, as we all know, and self-care is affection and kindness, only turned inward.

If you can't even think of what you should be doing to care for yourself, start with thinking about how you show your love to others. If you buy other people flowers, why not buy some for yourself? If you hug your friend when you can see she's having a bad day, why not comfort yourself in a similar way?

- Take care of your body. Are you well-fed, sleeping properly and staying healthy with exercise?

- Do you do enough activities that really make you happy and fulfill you? Why not?

- Do you eat crap, take nonsense from other people or routinely treat yourself badly?

- Do you get enough relaxation and rest throughout the day?

- Are you actively harming yourself with substances, negative self-talk or stress?

Today, try to baby yourself a little. Treating yourself after years of self-neglect can feel a little indulgent … but why can't you also be comfortable? Relaxed? Safe? Entertained? Whatever you do for yourself, make sure that it's communicating the message: "you are loved and lovable".

Day Seven: Kill the comparison habit

We live in a strange world. At no other time in human history has it been more commonplace to assume that *we're all special* and everyone is created equal and blah blah blah, and yet, at no point have people ever felt so bad about themselves.

We raise our children to believe that they're all amazing in their own special ways, and that nobody is better than anybody else. We are fanatic about policing people who suggest anything other than the most PC, all inclusive, liberal sentiments.

And yet.

If beauty was truly in the eye of the beholder, why would women spend the millions they do on cosmetics and plastic surgery? If we all truly believed that we're all special, why do we care so much about competitive sports, beauty pageants or handing out the Nobel Prize?

Here's another unpopular opinion: we are *not* all created equal. Some people are more far along their journey than others, some people are talented and some have a lot of work to do. We can't all be the best in everything we do. A quick scan of your immediate social circle will tell you conclusively that most people are just alright.

But, so what?

Here's the real radical self-love: people can be just alright ... and *still* lovable. Yup. You don't have to be a winner to be lovable. You don't have to be better than everybody else to deserve self respect. When it comes to love, there is no race, there is no prize.

Comparison to others is a slow, nasty way to die.

When you have compassion and kindness for yourself, it's not *because* of anything. It's not a Nobel Prize or a Miss Universe crown. It's just the baseline of acceptance and kindness you give yourself for doing the dirty work of being a human being.

You don't have to blow smoke up your own ass, if you'll pardon the expression. Lying to yourself and saying that you're perfect and beautiful just as you are is not going to be truly satisfying and worse, *it's not actually true*. But what's so great about beauty and perfection anyway? Self-love isn't about heaping on baseless compliments. It's about saying, "this is what I am, right now, and I accept that."

Many self help esteem books out there will just encourage you to swing the other way. While it's certainly unhealthy to say, "I'm overweight and so I'm unlovable", it's not much better than, "I'm perfect and beautiful as I am. In fact, I'm a *goddess* and much, much better than those other skinny bitches and it's just society that's brainwashed us all and you know what? It's time for my four o'clock self-care donut."

Real self-love is not encouraged much: "Yeah I'm a bit chubby. I could stand to lose some weight. I'm dedicated to being kind and compassionate to myself anyway while I work on it."

Real self-love encourages you to accept what is right in front of you, but that doesn't mean there is no room for improvement. In fact, a sober, kind look at your flaws makes it much easier to do what you need to and improve.

Today, have a look at all those things you compare about yourself. Look at them full on. Then say, "that's OK".

Day Eight: Don't hide who you really are

Self-hate is like walking around with a massive black blanket around on your head. Nobody can see you, or hear you speak, and you keep bumping into things and hurting yourself. If you've already made the unanimous decision that you are unworthy, your actions will naturally follow to confirm that belief. If your ideas are stupid, you're not likely to voice them, and if you believe you're a bit of a loser, why put yourself out there at all?

Taking off the blanket can be a bit scary, and leave you feeling a bit vulnerable, but with it on, you never truly connect with others. Today, take your lovely self out there for a spin and dare to be the real, authentic you that you are - not the ideal "real you" from the fashion magazine after a juice cleanse and a blowout, but the person you are *right now*, reading this book.

Allow yourself to be seen. Trust that while it's possible you'll be rejected, most likely you won't be, and in fact, when you dare to express yourself, interesting things happen. Be vulnerable, be a bit pushy, speak your mind and don't be afraid to be what you are. Challenge yourself today and try it!

Day Nine: Focus on your positive qualities

Your ego's job is to convince you that everything you already think is true.

This would be fine, if your assessments were always 100% correct ... but they usually aren't. When you are convinced that you are not lovable, not worthy, or *bad* in some way, your ego does its best to find evidence to support this belief.

Beliefs are active, and even though you may not notice yourself doing it, beliefs filter out information from the world until it looks like "reality". Even if that reality looks really bleak. Even if that reality isn't true.

I have a friend who has low self-esteem. When people say nothing, she assumes they're thinking the worst about her, but if they compliment her, she thinks "A ha! You're just saying that to make me feel better". In fact, her filter is so crappy that the more you compliment her, the more likely she is to think that you mean *exactly the opposite of what you say*. Does my poor self-esteem look big in this?

To counter this constant filtering that your pesky ego is doing on the sly, you'll need to *actively* start looking for evidence that goes against your beliefs about yourself. You need to start complimenting yourself ... and believing it!

Today, forget about being humble and get busy making a list of your positive qualities. Come on now, don't pout and pretend there aren't any! Even if you're feeling sulky and can't think of anything, start with "I survived infancy" and go from there.

Make a list of ten things that you love about yourself, big or small. Think of achievements, attributes you can be proud of, things you've made, fears and difficulties you've overcome, people's lives you've made

23

better, good jokes you've told or even the fact that in the right light, you look a little bit like Angelina Jolie.

PS: How did it feel to be so nice to yourself? Hey, I won't mind if you want to keep going after number ten...

Day Ten: Know what you like

You'd think that knowing what you like and moving towards it would be the easiest thing in the world, but look at anyone and I can guarantee they have some unfulfilled dream, some unexplored idea, some hobby they always wanted to try but never did.

Today, a short exercise in deliberately grabbing your own happiness by the horns.

Step one: make a nice, juicy list of all the things that make you happy in life. Again, don't put down things you're supposed to want, but look back on life and try to remember the things that actually made you happy.

With this little happiness inventory, you depend less on the outside world to make you happy and learn a valuable skill: how to make yourself happy. This can be working out, spending time with family, making art, baking, looking through old photographs, watching stand up comedy, dancing, long walks, a night out, a night in, certain people, a particular outfit that makes you feel like an utter fox, anything really.

Step two: lists mean nothing without action! Choose one (or three, who's counting) and actively make yourself happy today!

Day Eleven: Know what you *don't* like

Maybe this is cynical, but the main function of the media is not exactly to make you feel happy with yourself. Big corporations don't care if you're a good sister or if you have a rich inner life or if you're fighting a hard battle against low self-esteem. They just want to sell you as much crap as possible and if they do that by putting hooks deep into the most fragile parts of your psyche, well, it's business as usual right?

But, you have a choice.

If you can cultivate a sense of awareness and unshakeable belief in your own worth, you'll be able to just laugh at the lingerie ad and get on with your life, money and sanity intact. Fashion magazines, celebrity reality shows, shitty friends on Facebook - if they don't help, why are they in your life?

Today, a spring clean. If it tells you a story about how lame and unlovable you are, out it goes.

- That passive aggressive friend who just wants to give you "friendly advice" about how your hair looks stupid? *Out.*

- Parents who think your PhD is great and all, but did you know Jerry's neighbor's son just got his *second* PhD this year? You look thin. Anyway, when are you having children? Have you put on weight? *Out.*

- That newspaper article that provides conclusive evidence from a Stanford University study that shows that your spoilt, entitled generation sucks, like, *so much*, and that you'll all be renting and paying off student loans forever? *Out.*

- That "motivational" poster on Facebook of your friend's abs / holiday / baby that make you feel slapped in the face every time you check your phone? *Out.*

- That pair of teeny tiny jeans at the back of your closet that keep reminding you how far you are from your goal weight? *Out.*

- Those infomercials that seem to delight in telling you how dirty your children are or how saggy your breasts look or how outdated your smartphone is? *Out.*

- Your yoga teacher who condescendingly tells you that it's fine, he totally doesn't judge you for eating meat, but, it's a fact that vegans are better in bed and if you're fine with that who is he to judge? *Out.*

- That gym filled with mirrors? *Out.*

- That friend who keeps sending you self help books? *Out.*

Today, tune into all those things in life that work to undermine your confidence, your self-worth and your peace of mind. Take a scalpel to them and cut them right out. If you find yourself asking, "but what if my hair really *is* stupid?" then run don't walk - these things have overstayed their welcome for long enough.

Day Twelve: Reflect

In the beginning of this book, I asked you to have a go at rating your level of self-love. Today, you'll see if almost two weeks of concerted effort has made any difference. Rate your degree of self-love again, from 1 to 10.

What have you learnt about yourself? What patterns have you uncovered? If you and yourself were in a relationship, what would your Facebook status be? Would you be like that annoying couple who playfully argue over who loves each other the most or would you post status updates along the line of, "don't you just hate some people? I'm not going to say who but *you know who you are*"?

A warning

We live in a competitive world. People care about who's winning. But avoid the temptation now to see your "self-esteem" score as just another thing you have to do, just another thing to worry about being good enough at. The moment you're all like, "Ugh, I'm so bad at having self-love", then, well, it all evaporates.

If you started with a score of 5 and feel like you could bump it up now to a 6, don't write it off as a failure. Remember, you took a long time to be the person you believe you are today - it'll take a while to change that! Self-love can be a slippery thing to get a hold of if you're not used to it. Instead of judging yourself, try to practice a bit of self-compassion instead.

Day Thirteen: Self-talk

I used to have a friend that couldn't fall asleep at night unless the TV was on. In fact, he had become so used to the constant background noise in his bedroom at all times, that for him, he barely even noticed it anymore. If you turned the TV *off*, well, that was a different story.

Negative self-talk is like having a really, really bad TV show playing in the background of your life. For most sane people, having "Here Comes Honey Boo Boo" or "Keeping Up With the Kardashians" blaring in their living rooms 24/7 is more or less exactly what hell looks like. And yet, do it for long enough and you stop caring as much. You might even start to believe that the universe consists only of sassy, obese children and heavily made up women taking selfies of their asses.

Someone could try to turn it off one day or just change the channel to something a little nicer, but you'd be so far gone by then you'd say, "No! I can't sleep without it" like my friend.

Signs your self-talk is completely terrible, awful and no good

- You would never say the same thing to another person - and if you did, you might get smacked / ignored forever after.

- It's *emotional* content. For example, you don't tell yourself that you appear to be having a breakout and need some lotion, but rather that you're a hideous pizza-face and nobody could ever love a monster like you.

- It sounds suspiciously like negative things you've been told in the past by other people. It's sad, but sometimes an offhand insult from a decade ago morphs over the years, without you even noticing that you've just taken it on as your own now. Try saying your self-talk in the voice of a judgmental parent, an ex

29

or an enemy. Sound familiar?

- The things you tell yourself prevent you from acting, from reaching out to others or from trying to achieve your goals. Negative self-talk is usually the kind that convinces you to sit somewhere and sulk and fume, instead.

Why positive self-talk is overrated

Many self help books will treat your tender, complex brain a bit like a toaster or a router that's on the blink. Not working? Try whacking it a bit or switching it off and then on again. The idea with much of the positive thinking philosophy out there is that if you have a negative thought, you should just replace it with a *positive* one, rinse and repeat and hey, presto, you'll love yourself more and feel happy at last.

The trouble with this idea is that nobody wants to actually do it. And for good reason. If you're convinced you're too porky and hate that you can never wear sleeveless tops, the solution is not to keep telling yourself, "you're gorgeous! You have the upper arms of a supermodel!" and go ahead and wear sleeveless tops all day every day.

Too often, positive thinking = denial and delusion.

More soothing, more realistic and more satisfying is a *realistic* view. Glowing positivity may make you feel good for a short time, but if you're a rational person, you'll eventually look in the mirror and think, "Oh damn. That actually doesn't look flattering at all."

While negative self-talk is definitely not doing you any favors, unrelenting positivity with no basis in reality is just as bad, and in fact the two frequently encourage one another.

Instead, try constructive, realistic self-talk. You'll know it's constructive and realistic if it allows you to *accept* both the good and bad aspects of the reality in front of you, and move ahead with calm, focused action. Realistic self-talk is like turning off the damn TV and asking yourself, "now what was I doing again?"

Useless negative thought: "I'm too old for this studying shit. I could never get my Masters degree this late in life. I'm just doomed to wait out the rest of my life in a job I hate."

Useless positive thought: "You're a deeply wise and experienced human being who doesn't even need to go back to school because you're so beyond that now. In fact, what could university teach you that you don't already know?"

Useful realistic thought: "I missed my chance when I was younger to pursue further study. I'll be a bit rusty compared to my younger fellow students, sure, but I'm probably a lot more disciplined than them. I'm not getting any younger, and I don't want to waste any more time. I'm going to call and make an appointment with an advisor this afternoon"

The first two are just extreme, skewed perceptions of reality. The third may not impress a positive thinking guru but it will do something else: power you to be better. It might give you the courage to accept your limitations and work around them anyway. An overly negative view will immobilize you ...but so will an overly positive one.

Some schools encourage this kind of thinking in children: everyone gets a gold star, everyone is special, and there is no way to fail the course. But this robs children of the ability to confront their limitations head on. Which friend would you rather have - the honest but accepting one ("that color is amazing on you but I don't think those sleeveless shirts are doing you any favors") or the one who tells you you're amazing no matter what, so much so that you wonder if she's just lying through her teeth ("seriously! You make arm cellulite look so cute! You're perfect, don't you dare change or I'll literally have to kill you!")

Today, try to be curious about the nature of the self-talk that's going on in your head. Ask yourself, is it the kind of talk that is encouraging you to take beneficial, useful action in your life? Is it the kind of talk that makes you acknowledge your weaknesses without them making you feel bad, but also see the good in yourself and in the situations you find yourself in? Is it just pure emotion or is it more realistic?

Instead of criticizing - look for ways to improve. There's no point beating yourself up; try to improve or accept that you can't.

Instead of dwelling on ways to judge yourself - try to look realistically at both the good and bad aspects.

Instead of black and white, all or nothing thinking - find a middle ground.

Compassion for yourself isn't the same as telling yourself sweet little lies (I'm sure you know a few people just like this) but it's about being kind, however far along you are in your journey. It's OK to not be perfect. It's OK to struggle sometimes.

Day Fourteen: Keep challenging yourself

Self-love is a habit just like any other. And just like any other habit, it can be learnt. Earlier in this guide, we practiced thinking of ourselves in different ways, i.e. what would life be like if we loved ourselves? If you threw yourself into this exercise, you might have found yourself thinking things like, "If I wasn't so scared, I would enter that competition" or "If I thought I was worth more, I would dump that asshole who keeps cheating on me".

Once you start changing up your mental software, expect some interesting changes. Suddenly, you may find yourself trying things you wouldn't ordinarily try.

Today, see if you can deliberately push yourself to get out of your comfort zone and try on the life of someone who loves themselves. What counts as challenging, new and exciting will be different for each person. For one person, travelling alone to South America for a year long sabbatical might be a piece of cake, but calling their mom up to ask for some emotional support is gut-wrenchingly hard. For another person, they're comfortable negotiating a long-overdue pay rise but are mortified at the idea of buying themselves something that they really want.

- Try a new skill - you don't have to be talented or have a knack, just enjoy it and do your best. Languages, sports or a part time course - your decision.

- Travel. Sometimes being somewhere different can really open your eyes to new possibilities.

- Be kind to other people. You'd be amazed at how the compassion habit is contagious.

- Pick one thing that you won't try because you're afraid of failing. Then do it. Is failing as bad as you thought it was? Maybe, just maybe, you don't even fail...?

- Dare to do the things that you know you're good at - go ahead and boast a little, be a little proud. Why not?

Day Fifteen: Don't be so hard on yourself

Here's a bit of bubble-bursting news: when you love yourself, life isn't any easier. Nope, not one bit. Sorry. It's just the same actually: bad things happen, sometimes you mess up and there's still a 50% chance that when you drop your toast on the floor, it lands butter-side down.

But your attitude makes a difference when things *do* go wrong. If you've been fed a steady diet of "Smile smile smile! Say your affirmations! Think positive!" then you might be tempted to come down hard on yourself when things don't look so rosy. Here you are again, a failure stuck at square one. Your juice cleanse just ended up giving you diarrhea and you can't be bothered to meditate anymore because it's boring and you secretly hate it.

Time for an expectation readjustment!

An expectation is just a resentment waiting to happen. Expect things that are unrealistic and life will quickly remind you of what's what. You'll "fail". But often what looks like failure is just a sign that what you thought reality was and what it really is were just not perfectly aligned. If you expected yourself to lose half your body weight in 2 months and be competing in the Miss Universe pageant just because you switched to diet soda and took the stairs that one time, you haven't "failed" when you stay exactly the same. You've only been given a clue that your expectations weren't quite right.

A lot of the time, being "hard on yourself" is the punishment you give yourself for not meeting with sky-high expectations. It's the realization that you want something that is not realistic. Today, have a look at some of your goals and ask yourself if they really are realistic. The best thing, in some cases, is to let go of the goal completely.

Day Sixteen: Give yourself the gift of meditation

When people think of meditation, they usually think of *formal* meditation. You know the kind of thing. Sit on a cushion, think about nothing (including that! Don't think about thinking about nothing! Ok, sorry, don't be stressed. You're trying to hard. Stop thinking about it!).

But meditation, the *informal* kind, can be an amazing way to start giving yourself the sweet loving you deserve. Meditation is like a holiday for your brain. Meditation is like opening up a window in a stuffy room and taking a big, deep breath.

Here are some ways to bring some confidence and self-esteem boosting meditation techniques into your life. Choose one or make up your own and give it a try as today's exercise.

- Take a long walk. Focus on how good it feels to immerse in your senses. Isn't nature wonderful? Doesn't everything look so content to be alive? Trees don't feel guilty, or stress about their size. They just are the things they are.

- Spoil yourself to a new bar of fancy soap and have a long, hot, relaxing bath. Thank your body for all the things it's done for you. It doesn't matter what it looks like, for the time being, but isn't it amazing how far it's carried you in this world?

- Zone out with an activity, craft or sport you love. There's something very redemptive about getting lost in activity.

- Sit still. Listen to the wind, feel the weight of your limbs and watch whatever comes into your mind. Accept all of it, and let it come without any goal toward it. Stop striving and just be aware.

Formal meditation is all about deliberately making time in your schedule to sit and meditate, but the great thing about informal meditation is that when you get really good at it, it's not just something you add onto your life, it *is* your life. Practice finding bliss in the walk from your house to your car, in a piece of music, in the patterns the crumbs make on the floor as your toast falls butter-side down onto it, in the feeling of how warm and lovely the shower water is, or how amazing it feels to stretch after a long, stressful day.

Day Seventeen: Stop taking everything so damn seriously!

There's a word for being super robust and yet loose and adaptable. A word to describe being resilient to all the hell life can throw your way and yet keeping up good spirits and an attitude of playful acceptance. It's called humor!

For most people, humor is attractive in others because it signals something pretty serious: this person is *strong*. They're able to take what life dishes up and keep smiling instead of wallowing in misery and contemplation. They're not terribly hung up on the *shoulds* and *musts* of life and know how to have fun. Not taking yourself seriously, in other words, is very, very healthy.

Over-seriousness can take many forms, all of them boring and horrible. Seriousness is life stripped of its juice, of its essence. Being inflexible about what you *know* is true and never considering something different, getting offended easily when someone makes fun of you, getting upset when things don't go your way, feeling embarrassed or guilty too easily, sulking, stewing over yourself and your life problems intently, over analyzing things, being passive aggressive ...all of this is very serious and it's very, very boring.

Let loose, be a little silly, say "so what?" An interesting thing might happen. You may discover the things you fear are not that bad. That your problems are kind of small. That if you look at pain and confusion in life, it sometimes looks pretty funny. That none of us really knows what we're doing in this life, and it's totally bizarre, and it's OK.

Today, you're not going to take yourself seriously.

- Embarrass yourself. Make a cheesy joke, gush about your feelings or reveal a secret that makes you a bit bashful.

- Express yourself. Dance in the supermarket when you like the music, chat to strangers and answer honestly the next time someone asks how you are. Sing karaoke, chat up a cute stranger in a bar, wear that skirt that you're worried is too "out there", play on the swings in the playground.

- Play practical jokes on your friends, take a break and do exactly the thing everyone's least expecting you to do.

- Poke fun at yourself. We all have silly habits and beliefs.

- Being a grown up is so overrated. Go exploring somewhere you've never been before, break the rules or flirt with a stranger. Be a kid again.

Or, do whatever you want, I'm not the boss of you.

Day Eighteen: Journal

Today, lets take a moment to recap and see what we can see. The more you talk about things, share them and reflect on them, the more real they become. Today, take a journal and write down your thoughts and feelings about where you are right now. Be honest (don't worry - I won't judge you!) but try to be realistic too, rather than overly positive or negative.

What new habits have you started over these last few days that you enjoy and want to keep doing?

What habits are seeming more and more like they don't belong in your life?

What achievements have you made? What difficulties did you face and overcome?

In what ways were you lazy, afraid or just full of nonsense?

What is your plan to move forward without all of that baggage?

How can other people be a part of your self-love journey?

Which people are supporting your journey and which people are on a different journey? Could it be time to say goodbye to some fellow travellers and find others who fit your goals a bit better?

How did you deal with failure, boredom and doubt?

In what ways are you already exactly what you need to be?

In what ways do you want to be better?

Are there any sweet little lies you've been telling yourself that you're brave enough to let go of now?

Are your expectations realistic?

Could you actually be a little harder on yourself?

Is your lifestyle supporting this new picture of yourself, or sabotaging it?

Day Nineteen: Forgive yourself

Look at anybody around you and beneath their smiles and seemingly normal exterior, is someone who did something wrong once. Think about it. I'd bet you that every single person you meet was mean to an ex, or was wrong in an argument, or made some stupid decisions in High School or went out with frosty blue eyeshadow in the 90s. We've all said something we shouldn't have, broken something, offended someone, or done something so unspeakably unforgivable that we can scarcely even talk about it today.

And what other way could it be? As long as there are people who grow and change, there will also be mistakes, missteps, crimes, misdemeanors, misjudgments, missed opportunities and yes, regrets. You might feel fine about yourself right here and now, but when you look back at your past, think "oh my god" and silently withhold forgiveness.

So you walk around with a little scrapbook of guilt, shame, regret and embarrassment in your heart. Like hideous snapshots from your past, each page of this gross scrapbook makes you feel like a horrible person. This scrapbook is all about, "you should have..." or "if only you..." and when you flip through its pages, you cringe and feel bad.

As we've seen, though, people are usually much more forgiving when it comes to *other people's* transgressions. If you've been in any kind of long-term relationship, chances are you've forgiven your partner for being an ass that one time or constantly leaving their pajamas on the floor. When it comes to family, many people are even more forgiving: "that's just the way she is, it's OK, we all love her anyway."

Wouldn't it be nice if you could forgive yourself?

Forgiveness isn't:

- Allowing yourself to "get away with it"
- Pretending the problem isn't there or
- Only something you do when you don't care about it much.

In fact, forgiveness means the most when the transgression is the greatest. Forgiveness doesn't mean you're OK with the wrong you've done, but it *does* mean that you are committed to having compassion for yourself anyway.

Today, lets have a flip through that gruesome scrapbook. Open your mental catalogue of all your failures. Don't try to excuse your behavior - if you sucked, admit it. Own it and take responsibility. But life moves forward, not backwards. If you're wracked with guilt, ask yourself gently what you can do, right now, to be better and learn from your mistakes. If there's nothing you can do now, well, you have a mammoth task: self-forgiveness. Look at your past failings and regrets and say to yourself, "This was bad. But I forgive myself. I have compassion for myself and am trying to be better everyday."

Day Twenty: Reflect - again!

Man, you can just never do enough reflection.

For today, take your pick of the following exercises (choose whichever one resonates with you but don't be lazy!) and make a few scratchings in your journal.

- Write a letter to your old self, forgiving yourself for being a complete idiot and being kind for the path you were on - and *still are on*. Take the position of an older, wiser you. Be kind! We all make mistakes.

- Write a letter to someone in your life who is undermining your confidence and your ability to love yourself. Calmly assert your human right to love and respect, and claim your worth. I don't have to tell you to destroy this letter, but it may very well inspire you to make some changes when it comes to this person.

- Write an obituary for yourself after a life lived with dignity, self-love and compassion. What kind of person do you want to be? What do you imagine people will say about you when you shuffle off this mortal coil? Are you happy with that?

- Write yourself a pep talk letter to read when you're feeling low. You'd be amazed at how reassuring it is to read it later when you're feeling tired or uninspired. Remind yourself that ups and downs are normal, and that no matter what happens, you're committed to your experiences with compassion and kindness. You could call this, ahem, a self-love letter.

Day Twenty-One: Stay aware

Before you knew it, the 21 day challenge has almost come to an end. It doesn't take that long to form a new habit. But the key, of course, is to *keep going* after you finish this book. With a bit of luck, a bit of willingness to try something different and a lot of courage, you may have discovered that self-love is not only something that you need to nurture in your life, but something that you - yes *you* - are capable of, right now in this moment.

Self-love isn't something you get round to once the rest of your life is sorted out. It isn't a reward you give yourself for finally reaching some ever-shifting goals of what you should be. It isn't something nice in principle, but for other people and not you. Self-love is a habit, more than anything - just the same as self-hate is a habit.

Nothing in life survives without energy. To keep your budding self-love alive and well, it needs regular care, attention and maintenance. As if you were weeding a garden, you need to regularly rip out anything that is threatening it, too.

Ways to maintain your self-love

- Set up a morning or evening routine where you do ... whatever you need to feel good and grounded in yourself. Note: not permission to lay in bed or eat a second helping of pudding!

- Get into the habit of saying "thank you" when you receive a compliment. *And nothing else*. You don't need to blush and giggle and launch into a million reasons why you're actually awful and the other person must be brain damaged not to see it. Just "thank you" and move on.

- Try the wristband trick: put a band round your right wrist. Every time you catch yourself doing something against your commitment to self-love, move it onto the left side. The only way to get it back on the right side is to do something loving for yourself again. This is a great way to remind yourself to be kinder but also cuts you some slack. You don't have to be 100% self-loving, you just have to be more self-loving than you are self-hating.

- Reign in your criticism of others. Make it a habit to notice and compliment people on things, listen closely to them and when you find yourself angry at them, remind yourself of their good qualities. Develop this skill for others and you can't help but get some of the same attitude thrown your way. It's a win win.

- Set a morning intention. This is like a to-do list, but for your spirit! Decide what attitude you'll take that day and commit to it, no matter what. Imagine yourself accepting and overcoming the challenges of the day. Have trust in yourself that you have what's needed to be awesome that day, whatever life throws at you.

- Keep journaling. You can decide how frequently to add an entry. Watch out for turning it into a "dear diary", though. What you want is to keep close tabs on your self-talk, set goals for yourself and make sure you're holding yourself responsible to them, not bitch about things that are bugging you that day.

- Make self-care, grooming and "me time" a regular thing. Some people book a monthly massage, others spoil themselves to a little treat on the weekends, others make sure they have enough time each day to have a nice bath, do their hair and get their mindset straight for the day. Did you know that Japanese researchers have found that people who use cosmetics report higher levels of happiness? When you groom, primp or preen, you're telling yourself: I'm pretty. I'm worth it. I'm hot. I deserve to be cared for.

- Develop a backbone and learn to stand up for yourself against people who attack your worth. The best way to do this? With kindness. People who judge others harshly often turn the same standards on themselves, so you can be guaranteed they probably feel like shit a lot of the time, even if they don't show it. Have compassion and rise above it! "Ooh, are you sure you can wear that dress with your wide hips?" says your mother in law. You say, "Yes! I love my hips and this accentuates their wideness. Now, what were we talking about?"

- Share the struggle. It can be difficult to remember to maintain your new habits, but a lot easier if you enlist the help of caring friends. Chat to people you love and trust and explain that you're trying to love yourself a little more. You'd be surprised at how many people would be more than obliging to help. They're fans of yours, remember?

- Keep up a daily meditation or awareness exercise. All you need to do is notice yourself being negative and make a little space to do something different. This could mean regular nature walks, hot baths, art sessions or quietly gazing out the window.

Of course, it doesn't matter what you do, only that you keep at it consistently. How did you get a bad self-esteem in the first place? Well, that's a question for another book, but it probably happened slowly. You'll heal your sense of dignity the same way: slowly. Today, as your final act, commit to maintaining some affirming and loving habits every day.

Conclusion

Watch the look of horror and/or doubt that flashes across people's faces when you mention self-love and you have your proof for why we all need it so badly. The world is a complicated, busy place and many of us have sacrificed our peace of mind and feeling of being a worthy human simply from lack of effort.

Sad to say, but the world is at times not the most nurturing place. There is love and acceptance out there, but it more often than not begins *in here*. My hope is that with this book, you've found some easy, practical ways to take a moment, turn off the shitty mental TV and give yourself a big hug. Not because you're a winner or "deserve" it, but because you're a human being, doing this crazy work of being alive, and why not?

Self-compassion is easy. It's free (and much cheaper than therapy - yay!) and perhaps best of all, it's contagious. Sometimes, one of the bravest things we can do is to look into ourselves and say, *"self, you're OK"*. When we love ourselves (not some pretty magazine picture of our ideal selves, but our actual, real selves), we open ourselves up to loving others more deeply, too.

I don't know you, reader, but it's my sincere wish that at the end of this challenge, you're committed to bringing a little less hatred, fear and judgment into the world and want to go out there and bring love and acceptance instead.

Made in the USA
Lexington, KY
01 June 2018